Thank you God for our day
in the country

Eira Reeves

For Charlotte, my god-daughter

Scripture Union Publishing
London   Sydney

Katie and Mark live in the country. Today they went for a picnic.

Where do you go for picnics?

On the way they saw some birds, butterflies and bright flowers.

What colours are the flowers?

farm

They stopped to say hello to Winnie the horse and her new foal.

What would you name her foal?

In the next field, they saw some sheep eating grass and their lambs playing.

What do we get from sheep?

Katie and Mark went to a farm and met Farmer Hedges and his dog Shep.

What animals live on a farm?

They saw the hens. Farmer Hedges
gave them some fresh eggs.

How many eggs can you see?

Rob, the farmer's son, waved to them from his tractor.

What is in the trailer?

The pigs made a funny noise. It made Katie laugh.

What noise does a pig make?

'I'm hungry,' said Mark. So they sat down by a stream and ate their picnic.

What food can you see?

No Litter

On the way home, Mark made Katie a daisy chain. He put it on her head like a crown.

Can you make a daisy chain?

Outside their house they found a bird's nest. The baby birds were being fed.

How many birds can you see?

At bedtime Katie and Mark talked to God
and said, 'Thank you, God, for our day in
the country.'

What did you do today? Tell God about it.

© Eira Reeves 1988   First Published 1988   Reprinted 1991   All rights reserved
Published in the UK by Scripture Union, 130 City Road, London, EC1V 2NJ
Published in Australia by Anzea Publishers, PO Box 115, Flemington Markets, NSW 2129
ISBN 0 86201 467 0 UK   ISBN 0 85892 331 9 AUSTRALIA
Co-edition organised and produced by Angus Hudson Ltd, London.
Printed in England by BPCC Hazell Books, Paulton